# Ole & Sven's Bucket List

## Featuring

Bruce Danielson as Ole
and Bob Bergstrom as Sven

Adventure Publications, Inc.
Cambridge, MN

## Credits

Photography by Ryan Jacobson

Illustrations by Shane Nitzsche

Edited by Ryan Jacobson

Cover and book design by Jonathan Norberg

10 9 8 7 6 5 4 3 2 1

Copyright 2013 by Bruce Danielson and Bob Bergstrom
Published by Adventure Publications, Inc.
820 Cleveland Street South
Cambridge, MN 55008
1-800-678-7006
www.adventurepublications.net

Printed in the U.S.A.

ISBN: 978-1-59193-413-4

# Acknowledgments

Thanks to the following friends, neighbors and colleagues who appeared in the book: Page 13: Kenny Krona; Pages 16 and 24: Ann Berg; Page 46: Lois Salo, Carol Bell and Mary L. Hanson; Page 49: Char Jacobson; Page 56: Lois Tureen; Page 60: Jack Hammargren; Page 74: Joel B. Pennington; Page 89: Ryan Jacobson; Page 93: Michele LaHood and Kirstin Bruss.

Thanks to the following businesses and friends who lent supplies or locations and made this book possible: Menards of Cambridge; the James Sullivan family for use of the bikes; Cambridge-Isanti High School and Justin Kennedy for use of the instruments; Purple Hawk Country Club; Pine Brook Inn; White Castle; Cambridge Lutheran Church; Village Hair Parlor; Anoka-Ramsey Community College in Cambridge; Josh and Thea Lowman for use of their boat; Joel Pennington's Guitar Shop; and Total Wellness Coaching, LLC.

A special thank you to Ryan Jacobson for his excellent photography skills, his technical skills, his creative ideas and his extensive input into this book, which resulted in this finished product.

# Bruce Danielson's Dedication

God has blessed me and given me everything on my bucket list:

1) My wife of 41 years, Judy, who makes every day a joy to wake up to;

2) A terrific son, Matthew, who is an outstanding husband, father and teacher, having been named White Bear Lake Teacher of the Year and a semi-finalist for Minnesota Teacher of the Year;

3) A daughter-in-law, Jen, second to none, who is also a great teacher, a great wife and mother, and the best choreographer ever;

4) A wonderful granddaughter, Corinne Olivia Danielson, who delights us every time we see her (even though she learned to give her grandfather the raspberries);

5) The best friends a couple could have in Bob and Marj Bergstrom, and the chance to collaborate with one's best friend on this project;

6) The honor of being a finalist for the 2012 Minnesota Teacher of the Year along with nine of the best teachers Minnesota has to offer;

7) The honor to have served in the Minnesota Army National Guard for 33 years with some of the greatest soldiers/colleagues that one could hope to know.

I am eternally grateful and dedicate this book to all of those mentioned here. I wish for all of you readers that you be as blessed as I have been and achieve all the items on YOUR bucket list.

# Bob Bergstrom's Dedication

Life can be fun, and life can be tough. As most families do, my family has experienced both sides of life through the years. This book is silly and fun, and that's the side of life I want to celebrate.

I'm almost always silly and fun with my fabulous grandkids, so I dedicate this book to them: Chille, Renata and Sonja.

My busy adult children and daughters-in-law perhaps think I'm silly and fun too often, so I dedicate this book to them: Alison, Sam and Kari, and Scott and Jana.

And my lovely and patient wife, Marjo, says she loves the silly and fun side of me, so I dedicate this book to her.

My loving family . . . together, we've looked at life from both sides . . . May we enjoy more of life's fun and silliness! I love you all!

## Foreword (by Ole)

Believe it or not, I convinced Sven dat I vould do da Foreword and he should do da Backward. Anyvay, as we all get older, it just makes sense dat we vould start to tink about da tings we vant to do before we . . . vell, let's just say, "before we become 'American Idle.'" So we decided to do one of da tings on our bucket list and write a book together. Vat a surprise ven Sven and I both had da same favorite number: 164. We decided to put together 164 different tings dat people should try to do vile above ground. Dere are boxes for you to check off ven you've done dese tings, so we hope you like our list, and most of all, we hope you read our book and . . .

ENJOY

. . . to years many ,many have you may and ,book my and Ole's read and back sit So .list bucket your on tings do to time more even you give vould dat and ,lives our to time add we laugh we time every dat say dey because laugh you makes book dis hope We .yet in colored not three da of one only da is it because special is it But .books three of total grand a to library my bringing ,library home my to book dis add to excited am I .it did we But .one write less much ,pages 100 nearly of book a read could I thought never I .Ole vit book dis write to chance da had I dat glad so am I

(Sven by) Backward

# Get in Shape

## ■ #1 Participate in a Triathlon

Sven:  I see vy dey call it a TRI-athlon. I am really trying!

Ole:  Dere's nobody more trying dan you, Sven!

☐ **#2 Take Part in a Marathon**

Ole: Vipe my brow, Sven. Marathons are exhausting!

# #3 Work Out Daily

Sven: I woke up early vit da urge to exercise.

Ole: I hope you stayed in bed until dat urge vent away.

# #4 Learn to Swim

Ole: Swimming is really good for you.

Sven: Especially if you're drowning.

# #5 Take Long Bicycle Rides

Ole and Lena were riding up a big hill on their bicycle-built-for-two.

Ole: Lena, I'm too tired. I can't pedal any furder.

Lena: Den it's a good ting I kept da brakes on all da way up. Otherwise, we vould've slid back down, huh, Ole?

# Appreciate Music

■ #6 Conduct an Orchestra

Ole: Dinner time!

# #7 Start a Band

Ole was shopping in an old music store.

      Ole:  I'll take da red trumpet and dat accordion over dere.

  Owner:  You can have the fire extinguisher, but the radiator has to stay.

# #8 Learn to Play the Violin

What do a lawsuit and Sven's violin have in common?

We're much happier when the case is closed.

# #9 Learn to Play the Trumpet

What do Sven's trumpet playing and Mike Tyson have in common?

Both are hard on the ears!

# #10 Learn to Play the Organ

Sven: Vy is an organ recital like a religious experience?

Ole: In its playing, we sense da majesty of God. In its ending, we know His divine mercy, as we tank God it's over!

# #11 Learn to Play the Bagpipes

Sven: Ole, vy do you tink bagpipe players march ven dey play?

Ole: Dat's easy. Dey're trying to get away from da music!

# #12 Learn to Play the Oboe

Lena: Ole, quit playing dat oboe and answer me dis: Vat's da difference between an oboe and an onion?

Ole: I don't know, Lena. Vat?

Lena: No one cries ven you cut up an oboe.

# Improve Your Social Life

## ■ #13 Join a Country Club

Club Member:  No, you absolutely cannot join!

Sven:  Vy not? Are you afraid we'd raise a racket?

## #14 Buy a House

Banker: How much can you afford to pay per month?

Ole: About a tousand dollars.

Banker: Will you be getting fire and theft insurance?

Ole: I don't need dat. Vy vould a guy be robbing my house vile it's on fire?

## #15 Maintain a Positive Attitude

Sven fell off a tall building while cleaning windows, but he's such an optimist. As he passed the fifth floor, they heard him say, "So far, so good!"

## #16 Go on a Movie Date

Lena: Ole, dat love scene was really good. Does it make you vant to kiss like dose actors did?

Ole: Lena, do you know how much dey got paid to do dat?

# #17 Throw a Big Party

Ole: I'm going to throw a huge party and invite all my friends!

Sven: Ole, I'm already here.

# #18 Spend More Time with Friends

Ole attended a friend's party, where an amateur hypnotist was hired for entertainment. Ole volunteered to be hypnotized.

The hypnotist started swinging the gold watch, and Ole was asleep in no time. But just when he was ready to give Ole his first direction, the watch slipped from his hand and fell to the floor. It broke into a hundred pieces.

The hypnotist exclaimed, "Crap!"

It took two weeks to clean the living room.

# Change Your Eating Habits

■ #19 Become a Vegetarian

Ole: Wait, vegetarians don't eat VAT?

# #20 Try Lutefisk

Ole walked up to the counter and ordered lutefisk.

> Employee: You must be Norwegian.
>
> Ole: Vell, dat is a stereotype, isn't it? Just cuz I order someting Scandinavian, you decide I must be Norvegian. Dat is very offensive!
>
> Employee: Sorry to upset you, but I didn't decide you were Norwegian from your order of lutefisk. I decided you were Norwegian because this is a hardware store.

# #21 Learn the Four Food Groups

> Ole: It took me forty years to learn da food groups, but according to Lena, here dey are: fast, frozen, instant and chocolate!

# #22 Eat at Restaurants More Often

Ole and Sven walked into a fast food restaurant, pulled out their lunch bags and started to eat. An employee approached them and said, "You can't eat your own food in here." So they switched sandwiches.

# #23 Invite People to Dinner

Ole: Cuz of Lena's cooking, we never ask, "Guess who's coming to dinner." Nine times out of ten, it's da paramedics.

# #24 Experiment with Food

Ole: Lena, I suggested to your mudder dat she stick vinegar in her ear.

Lena: Vat for, Ole?

Ole: Cuz den she'd have "pickled hearing."

## #25 Taste Every Snow Cone Flavor

Sven: Ole, dis doesn't taste like lemon.

# Start a New Hobby

■ #26 Learn Origami

Sven: Keep folding. One of dese is bound to be a crane!

# #27 Build a Kayak

Ole's uncle Tunile built a kayak, but he wanted to use it in the winter. He built a fire in it to keep warm. Of course, it burned to ashes. Tunile had to swim to shore, thus proving, "You can't have your kayak and heat it too."

# #28 Learn to Juggle

A man was driving down the road when a highway patrolman pulled him over because his license plate tabs had expired. The patrolman noticed that the driver had an enormous amount of knives in the backseat, which was very suspicious. He asked why the man had such an abundance of knives.

The driver explained that he was a juggler, headed to a party where he would entertain people with his hobby.

The policeman doubted his story and asked him to demonstrate. The man got out the knives and started juggling four and five of them at a time. He was very, very good at it.

Right then, Ole and Sven drove by. Ole shook his head and said, "If dat's da new sobriety test, I quit drinking right now!"

# #29 Go Fishing

Lena: Cook a man a fish and you feed him for a day, but teach a man to fish and you get rid of him for da whole weekend!

# #30 Take up Gardening

Lena: Ole, it's supposed to help if you talk to da plants.

Ole: If dey don't talk back, are dey mums?

# #31 Learn Wine Appreciation

Sven: I've always vanted to learn to appreciate wine.

Ole: Dat's simple. Just get married.

## #32 Become a Magician

Sven tried a magic act where he cut his assistant in half. She got nervous and left the act. She moved to Toledo and Fargo.

# Volunteer More

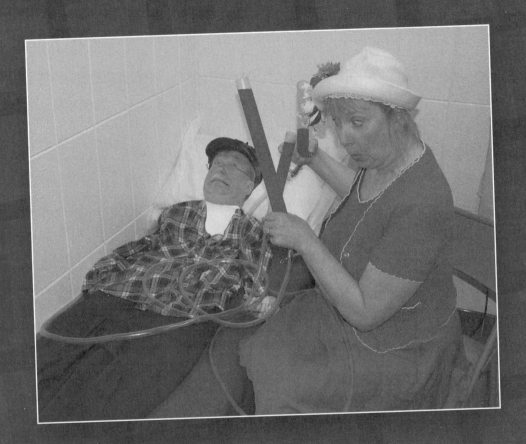

## ■ #33 Give Blood

Ole: Was I supposed to say, "Ven"?

## #34 Help Your Community

Ole and Lena weren't too impressed with Little Lena's new boyfriend. He wore a leather jacket, motorcycle boots and had tattoos all over his body. Ole decided to have a talk with his daughter.

> Ole: Little Lena, I don't tink dis boy is good for you. He doesn't seem very nice.

> Little Lena: Wanna know how nice he is? He told me he's doing 5,000 hours of community service!

## #35 Help Someone with a Difficult Customer

On a flight back home, Lena sat in First Class one time by accident. The flight attendant came and told her to move to the Coach section, but Lena refused. She said, "I'm an American. I'm an Olson, and I'm flying to Minot, Nort Dakota."

No matter how they tried to move her, she kept saying the same thing over and over. Finally they went to Ole and asked him to help. He whispered something in Lena's ear, and she immediately got up and moved to Coach. They asked Ole how he did it, and he said, "I told her dat First Class wasn't going to Minot."

# #36 Help a Sick Friend

Lena was at home feeling ill, when she received a telephone call.

> Lena: I'm sick. Everyting hurts. It could be da flu.
>
> Friend: Let me come over and make you dinner.
>
> Lena: Vould you do dat?
>
> Friend: I'll pick up some groceries and stop by. What does Sid like to eat?
>
> Lena: Sid? My husband is Ole.
>
> Friend: Oh, I must have the wrong number.
>
> Lena: Does dat mean you're not coming over?

# #37 Save Someone's Soul

A man collapsed on the street with what looked like a heart attack. Someone called for a priest to give him last rites. Ole stepped forward saying, "I'm not a priest, but I grew up across da alley from da Catholic Church. I've heard enough chanting from da church dat I could say some words over dis man." The crowd encouraged him to try, so he chanted, "B-4, I-19, N-38, G-54, O-72."

#38 Start a Movement

# Visit Exotic Places

☐ #39 Go to a Castle

## #40 Visit Rome

Ole and Sven have always wanted to take a trip to Rome—probably because they love to tell these jokes:

Sven: Do you know how to cut Rome in half?

Ole: Vit a pair of Caesars.

Sven: Do you know vat a forum is?

Ole: A 2-um and a 2-um.

## #41 Fly Around the World

Ole loves this story about his rich relative, Svensgard:

Svensgard: I'd like my carry-on to go to London, my suitcase to go to Tokyo and my garment bag to go to Istanbul.

Ticket Seller: Sir, we can't do that.

Svensgard: Vy not? You did it last time.

# #42 Visit Hawaii

> Ole: Honolulu is a great place to vacation: sand for da kids, sunshine for Lena and sharks for my mudder-in-law.

# #43 Attend the Summer Olympics

Sven, Ole and Torvald wanted to see the Summer Olympics. They did not have tickets, so they pretended that they were athletes in order to get in.

Torvald picked up a barbell. As he walked through the gate, he said, "Weightlifting," and they let him in.

Ole picked up a manhole cover. As he walked through the gate, he said, "Discus," and they didn't stop him.

So Sven went over and picked up a roll of barbed wire. As he went through the gate, he said, "Fencing."

# Learn a New Sport

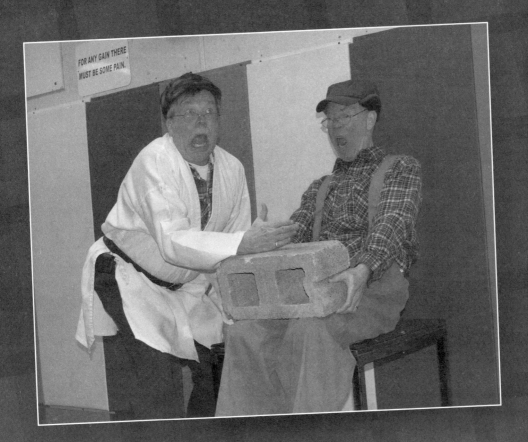

## ■ #44 Take Karate Lessons

Ole: Vy do I need to know dis? Ven vill I ever be attacked by a concrete block?

## #45 Take up Hunting

Ole went to a local nursing home to interview a legendary tiger hunter. Ole asked the old man to tell him the most frightening experience he'd ever had.

The old man said, "Once, I was hunting Bengal tigers in the jungles of India. Suddenly the largest tiger I ever saw leaped onto the path in front of me. He came toward me with a mighty ROARRR! I soiled myself."

Ole said, "I don't blame you a bit. I vould have done da same."

The hunter said, "No, not then. Just now, when I went ROARRR!"

## #46 Swim Long Distances

Ole tried long-distance swimming and somehow ended up on a lonely, tropical shore. As he stood up, he noticed his hands were purple. He looked at his feet, and they were purple. Worried, he unzipped his wetsuit. His chest and stomach were purple too. With his head in his hands, he cried, "Oh, no, I've been marooned!"

## ☐ #47 Go Horseback Riding

Sven: How could dey raise da price to 50 cents?
It's called a QUARTER horse!

## #48 Learn to Catch and Throw a Frisbee

> Ole: I was wondering vy da Frisbee was getting bigger . . . and den it hit me.

## #49 Play Baseball

Ole tried pitching, but his problems always started at the same time in every game: right after the National Anthem.

## #50 Become a Better Golfer

> Sven: Da doctor told me to play 36 holes a day, so I bought a harmonica.

## #51 Master Karate

Sven had a black belt in karate. He wasn't that good; he just never washed it.

# Appreciate Nature

## ■ #52 Go Stargazing

Sven: Ole, I can't see any stars.

Ole: Ya, but at least dere aren't any bugs.

# #53 Become a Bird Expert

Ole was taking an ornithology class to study birds at Fargo U. He was studying hard and learning a lot, hoping to impress the teacher and Lena. He was quite surprised when the test on birds turned out to be ten stuffed birds on the table, each covered with a sack so only its legs were showing. The students had to identify each bird by the shapes and markings on the birds' legs.

Ole was furious. This was not the test he was expecting. He marched up to the professor's desk, crumpled up his paper and threw it on the desk. Ole blew up at him, "Vat a ridiculous test! How could anyone tell da difference between dese birds by looking at dere legs? Dis exam is a rip-off!"

As Ole stomped out of the class, the professor called out, "Wait a minute, sir. What's your name?"

Ole turned, pulled up his pants legs and yelled, "You tell me, Teach! You tell me!"

## #54 Witness a Baby Being Born

Ole: I hope it's not a doubleheader!

# #55 Become a Farmer

Lena: Ole, we have to get a proper scarecrow to scare da birds away.

Ole: Are you kidding? Da one we got is so scary, da crows are bringing back da corn dey took last year. Vy should we get a new one?

Lena: Cuz my mudder's arms are getting tired.

# #56 Raise Farm Animals

On the farm one day, Ole said to Sven, "My mule is having fits. I remember dat your mule had dem too. Vat did you do?"

Sven replied, "I gave him a mixture of turpentine and kerosene."

So Ole went home and tried that, but his mule died.

The next time Ole saw Sven, he said, "I tried vat you told me, turpentine and kerosene, and my mule died!"

Sven shrugged his shoulders and said, "Ya, it killed mine, too."

# Start a New Hobby, Part 2

## ☐ #57 Knit Something

Sven: Real Norvegians don't just use yarn. I'm using steel wool to knit myself a toaster!

# #58 Learn a Foreign Language

Lena insisted that Ole take a French class. He was totally confused by all the new words. The teacher tried to encourage him by saying that he'd know he was making progress if he started dreaming in French.

The next day, Ole excitedly told the teacher that everyone in his dream the night before was speaking French.

"Good!" said the teacher. "What were they saying?"

Ole replied, "I have no clue. I couldn't understand a word of it!"

# #59 Read More Self-Help Books

At a bookstore, Sven asked the clerk, "Where is da self-help section?"

The clerk replied, "If I tell you, it will defeat the purpose, won't it?"

# #60 Study a World Atlas

Sven was studying a map of the Middle East while eating his mashed potatoes. Suddenly, his cat jumped up and startled him. He now has the only map of Turkey that's covered with gravy!

## #61 Take up Archery

Ole: See, Sven? Hitting a bull's-eye is easy!

# #62 Go Camping

Ole and Lena were camping in the woods, but the mosquitoes were terribly thick. So Ole went and changed into a clown outfit.

Lena asked, "Ole, vy are you dressed as a clown?"

Ole replied, "Everybody knows mosquitoes don't bite clowns, Lena. Dey taste funny."

# #63 Write a Magazine Article

Ole: I finally wrote someting dat was accepted by a magazine: a check for my yearly subscription.

# #64 Finish a Difficult Jigsaw Puzzle

Ole: Are you sure you have enough time to put dis puzzle together?

Sven: Ya, Ole, it shouldn't take more dan a few weeks.

Ole: I don't know, Sven. Da box says, "3 to 5 years."

# Do Something Nice for Others

## ■ #65 Bake a Cake for Someone

Sven: Dis file is for my uncle in Sing Sing. He
says he needs more iron in his diet.

## #66 Do a Good Deed Every Day

A van broke down while taking a family of penguins to the zoo. Sven offered to take them the rest of the way in his car. To the driver's surprise, he saw Sven driving the penguins again the next day.

Driver: I thought you were taking those penguins to the zoo!

Sven: Ya, I did. We had such a good time dat today I'm taking dem out for ice cream.

## #67 Help a Person in Need

Ole and Sven enrolled in a Community Education course. None of the students in class were very bright. They kept getting everything wrong, and soon the teacher became very frustrated. The teacher exclaimed, "Class, what's wrong with you? Are you idiots? I want everyone in this room who considers themselves an idiot to stand up."

Ole and Sven stood up.

The teacher asked, "So you consider yourselves idiots?"

Sven replied, "No, but we hated to see you standing alone."

## #68 Help a Stranger

Ole's father lost his false teeth while eating at a restaurant. The person at the next table offered him a spare set from his pocket.

Ole: How nice of you. Are you a dentist?

Stranger: No, a mortician.

## #69 Save Someone from Drowning

Sven had trouble while swimming, so he called to Ole to throw him a lifesaver.

Ole called back, "Do you vant cherry or grape?"

## #70 Always Tell the Truth

Lena accidentally took six peaches from the grocery store, so the judge sentenced her to six days in jail: one day for each peach she took.

Ole jumped up and exclaimed, "Judge, don't forget dat she took a bag of peas, too!"

# Make Religion a Priority

## ■ #71 Attend a Religious Retreat

Minister: Let us pray—that those two stay asleep.

# #72 Read the Bible

Ole: Ven Adam got together vit Eve, he didn't have a mudder-in-law. No wonder dat place was paradise!

# #73 Spread the Gospel

Ole: Ole Junior vants to marry his girlfriend.

Sven: Are you worried dat she's an atheist? She doesn't believe in God or in Hell.

Ole: Once she marries Ole Junior, she'll change her mind.

# #74 Always Act as You Would in Church

On a recent flight that Ole was on, the plane's engine went out. Since it looked like the plane might crash, the flight attendant ran to a priest on board and said, "Quick, do something religious!"

So the priest immediately walked up and down the aisle, taking up a collection.

## #75 Pray More Often

Sven was on an ocean cruise when suddenly the ship was in danger of sinking. The steward came running to the priest on board, saying, "Are you a person who believes in the power of prayer?"

The priest responded, "Yes, of course."

The steward replied, "Good, because we're one life preserver short."

## #76 Believe in Prayer

Torvald heard that prayer was powerful and could help those in need. He decided to give it a try, so he approached the pastor.

Torvald said, "Pastor, could you pray for my hearing?"

The pastor replied, "Yes, my son." He immediately stuck his finger in Torvald's ear and said a beautiful prayer. When he was finished, he asked Torvald, "Is it better? Can you tell a difference?"

Torvald answered, "How vould I know? Da hearing isn't until next Wednesday."

# Take Better Care of Yourself

## ■ #77 Get a Beauty Makeover

Beautician: I'm sorry sir, but in your case, this is the
best I can do.

# #78 Make Healthy Choices

Ole: I heard dat running kills germs, but how do you get dose little buggers to run?

# #79 Lose Twenty Pounds

Lena: Ole, how am I ever gonna lose weight?

Ole: Try da paint store, Lena. You can get thinner dere.

# #80 Stay Regular

Sven wrote to a mail-order company asking about the price of their toilet paper. They wrote back and told him to look on page 287 of their catalog.

Sven replied, "If I still had da catalog, I vouldn't need da toilet paper!"

## #81 Take Long Walks Daily

Ole, Torvald and Sven were planning a long walk in the desert. Ole said, "I'll bring an umbrella to give us shade from da hot sun."

Torvald added, "I'll bring sunglasses to protect our eyes from da sun's glare."

Sven said nothing, but the next day he showed up carrying a car door.

Ole asked, "Sven, vy are you bringing dat?"

Sven replied, "So I can open da window ven it gets too hot."

## #82 Live to a Ripe Old Age

Ole's grandpa said that a good way to live a long life was to mix a little gunpowder into your oatmeal every morning. When he died at the age of 93, he left 14 children, 28 grandchildren, 35 great-grandchildren and one 15-foot hole in the wall of the crematorium.

# Go Back to School

## ☐ #83 Take a College Course

Ole: I hope I'm ready, Sven. Da professor said
dere was going to be a make-up exam.

## #84 Take a Psychology Class

On the first day of class, Sven got nervous as the professor asked some beginning questions:

Professor: Lenny, what's the opposite of joy?

Lenny: Sadness.

Professor: Good. And John, what's the opposite of depression?

John: Elation.

Professor: Fine. Now, Sven, what's the opposite of woe?

Sven: I believe dat vould be "giddy up!"

## #85 Take a Biology Class

Ole took a biology class at Fargo U. The professor was making a point.

Professor: When I stand on my head, more blood runs into my head, and it makes my face turn red. So why is it that I'm standing upright and blood isn't causing my feet to turn red?

Ole: I know! It's cuz your feet ain't empty.

#86 Become a History Buff

## #87 Become a Teacher

Ole: Ven I was your age, I could name all da presidents.

Youngster: Yeah, but back then there had only been two of them.

## #88 Study to Be a Lawyer

Sven was in big trouble, so he hired Ole as his attorney.

Ole: Judge, my client has been accused of picking pockets. I know you vant to fine him $100, but he only has $75. Could you allow him a few minutes in da crowd?

## #89 Learn Sign Language

Ole: Every time I drive, people make strange gestures at me. I'll study sign language to learn vat dey're saying.

## #90 Learn to Fly a Plane

Control Tower: Mr. Olson, please give us your position.

Ole: I'm sitting in da cockpit. Where else vould I be? Uffda!

# Self-Improvement

## ■ #91 Take an Etiquette Class

Sven: I thought you said an "eat it quick" class!

## #92 Follow Instructions Better

Ole: Sven, vy were you crawling across da street?

Sven: Da sign said, "Don't walk."

## #93 Keep Up-to-Date on Current Events

Ole: Sven, did you hear about da little person who had his pocket picked?

Sven: Who could stoop so low?

## #94 Get a Part-Time Job

Sven took a job at a garden center. One day, the boss overheard him telling a customer, "We haven't had any, and I don't know if we'll ever get any again." After the customer left, the boss scolded Sven.

Boss: Never tell a customer we can't get something for them!

Sven: Sorry, boss. It von't happen again.

Boss: What was the customer looking for?

Sven: Rain.

## #95 Make Friends with Five Strangers

Ole: May I use your "cell" phone? Sven, dey don't get it.

Sven: Ole, I tink WE'RE about to get it!

# #96 Stimulate Your Mind by Playing Chess

Ole went to the local library where there was a chess tournament in progress. He was amazed to see a man playing chess against his dog, a beautiful border collie.

Ole waited until the game was over, and then he said to the owner, "Vat a smart dog! Where did he ever learn to play chess?"

The owner replied, "Smart? He's not that smart. I beat him three games out of four."

# #97 See a Marriage Counselor

Ole and Lena went to a marriage counselor, and one of the first things the counselor told Ole to do was to kiss Lena passionately.

Ole said he really didn't know what that word meant, so the counselor took Lena in his arms and kissed her for a long time. "See?" he told Ole. "She needs that at least four times a week."

Ole thought for a minute and replied, "Okay, vell, I can bring her in here on Mondays, Wednesdays and Fridays. But on Thursdays, you'll have to come to da house, cuz I go fishing."

# Overcome Your Fears

## ☐ #98 Make Peace with Your Enemies

Ole:  I tink my mudder-in-law vants to make
PIECES vit me!

# #99 Sing a Song in Public

Sven: I can't find anyone to sing vit me.

Ole: No problem. Just get a duet-yourself kit.

# #100 Laugh in the Face of Death

Ole and Sven had a friend opening a business, so they sent him flowers. But when the flowers arrived, the card said, "Rest in peace."

Ole called the florist to complain but was met with this explanation: "We're sorry, but imagine how the family at the funeral felt. They received your card that read, 'Congratulations on your new location!'"

# #101 Climb to High Places

Ole: Sven fell off da eaves of da house today.

Lena: Vat was he doing up dere?

Ole: Eavesdropping.

## #102 Overcome Your Fear of Snakes

Ole was in the movie theater when he looked at the seat next to him and saw a snake sitting there. In an effort to hide his fear, he tried to make conversation with it. "Excuse me, but I gotta admit: I'm kinda surprised to see you sitting in dis movie theater," said Ole.

"You're surprised?" said the snake. "I'm really surprised! I liked the book so much better. I should've left a half hour ago."

## #103 Overcome Your Fear of Dentists

Sven had to have a tooth removed, but he couldn't resist saying to the dentist, "Vat? You charge $200 for just two minutes of work, pulling out my tooth?"

The dentist replied, "I can extract it slower if that's what you want."

## #104 Overcome Your Fear of Spiders

Ole: Sven, I'm having trouble tinking of a spider joke.

Sven: Really, Ole? Dey are all over da web!

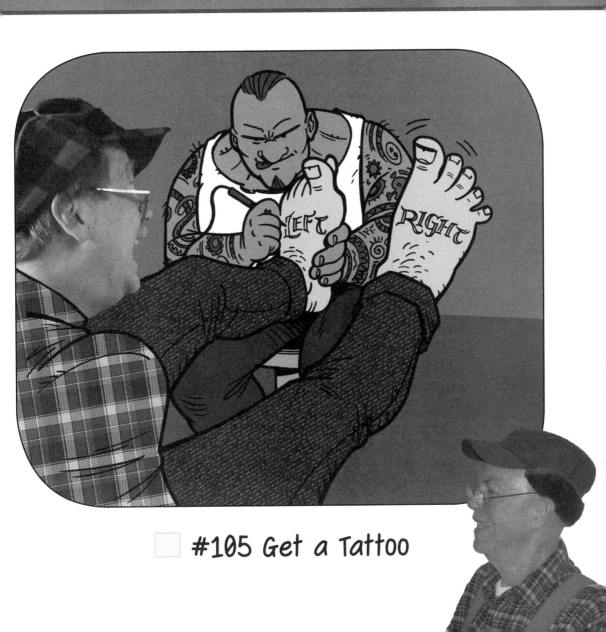

#105 Get a Tattoo

# Take a Memorable Vacation

## ■ #106 Take a Vacation Cruise

Sven: So, where's da buffet?

## #107 Stay in a Fancy Hotel

Sven was on vacation and called the hotel manager.

Sven: Dere's no door to get out of dis room.

Manager: There must be. You got into the room.

Sven: Vell, dere's a bathroom door, a closet door and a door dat I haven't tried yet.

Manager: Why not?

Sven: It says "do not disturb" on it.

## #108 Take a Long Road Trip

Ole and Lena were taking a long drive through Wisconsin, and they saw a sign advertising the town of Oconomowoc. They argued and argued about its pronunciation.

When they finally got to the town, they pulled into a fast food restaurant and said, "Before we order, could you settle someting for us? Tell us real slow where we are."

The waitress answered, "Burrr Gerr Kiinnggg."

## #109 Take a Hot Air Balloon Ride

Sven: Hey, Ole! If da flight offers a drink, try a "light" beer.

# #110 Go Fishing in the Ocean

Ole and Sven were fishing off the Florida coast. Their boat capsized, and they clung to it, afraid to swim to shore because of the dangerous Florida alligators.

Ole saw an old beachcomber walking along the shore and shouted to him, "Are dere any gators around here?"

The old guy replied, "Naw, they ain't been around for years."

Feeling much safer, Ole and Sven started swimming to shore. When they got about halfway there, Ole yelled to the guy again, "How did you get rid of da gators?"

The beach veteran chuckled. "Oh, we didn't do nuthin'. All the sharks got 'em!"

# #111 Travel to Historic Cemeteries

Ole was walking through a cemetery one evening when he started to imagine noises and movement behind him. He picked up the pace, but the noises seemed to speed up too. Finally, he hid behind a tombstone and yelled, "I don't know who you are. But if you're da devil, don't hurt me cuz we're related. I married your sister!"

# Enter a Contest

## ☐ #112 Participate in a Singing Contest

Judge: Your singing is like a pirate. You just
committed murder on the high C's.

## #113 Write a Prizewinning Movie Script

Ole: Which screenplay did you enter in da contest?

Sven: I decided on da one dat's called "Constipated."

Ole: Oh, I don't remember dat one.

Sven: Dat's cuz it hasn't come out yet.


## #114 Play in a Public Recital

After Sven performed in a violin recital, one judge asked the other, "What do you think of his execution?"

The other judge replied, "I'm in favor of it."


## #115 Enter a Beauty Contest

Ingeborg: I spend hours looking in da mirror at my beauty. Vould you call dat vanity?

Judge: No, I'd call that a vivid imagination!

# #116 Enter a Fishing Contest

Ole and Sven decided to enter an ice fishing contest, so they began searching for a good spot. All of a sudden, Ole said, "Dis looks like a great place to drill our hole."

A loud voice boomed from above, "There are no fish there!"

Ole and Sven looked up to the sky in amazement, wondering where the voice came from. Ole said, "I guess I was wrong. Let's try over dere."

Again the voice boomed, "There are no fish there!"

This kept up for more than an hour until Ole, a little spooked, looked up and said, "Are you God?"

The voice replied, "No, I own this skating rink and there are no fish here!"

# #117 Be a Contestant on a Game Show

Host: For $1000, name the most common crime among transvestites.

Sven: Male fraud?

# Read More

## ☐ #118 Publish a Bestseller

Ole: Uffda! Who vould ever buy dis book?

Sven: Even if dey did, dey'd never get dis far!

## #119 Read More Classic Literature

Sven was excited about reading *The Hunchback of Notre Dame* when he found it at the library, but he quit reading when he realized that it wasn't about football.

## #120 Read Biographies of Famous People

Sven: I just finished reading *The Life of Thomas Jefferson*.

Ole: Was it good?

Sven: No, it made me sad. He died at da end!

## #121 Read Books Out of Your Comfort Zone

Ole read a book by a famous fortune teller. He liked it so much that he decided to call her:

Ole: Could you help me remove a curse put on me years ago?

Fortune Teller: Maybe. Do you remember the exact words used?

Ole: I remember some of da words. It ended vit, "I now pronounce you man and wife!"

# #122 Share a List of Your Favorite Books

Ole and Sven's Top 10 Favorite Books:

#10: *Who Saw Him Go?* by Wendy Leave

#9: *Nothing's Ever Right* by Mona Lott

#8: *100 Miles to the Bus Stop* by Willy Makit (edited by Betty Wont)

#7: *Don't Wake the Baby* by Elsie Cries

#6: *Beginning Magic* by Beatrix Star

#5: *Falling from a Window* by Eileen Dowt

#4: *Improve Your Target Shooting* by Mr. Completely

#3: *The Most Embarrassing Moment* by Lucy Lastic

#2: *The Insomniac* by Eliza Wake

#1: *Apologizing Made Thimple* by Thayer Thorry

# Appreciate Music, Part 2

## ☐ #123 Learn to Play Guitar

Ole: I'm returning dis guitar. It has a big hole in da middle.

# #124 Learn to Appreciate Country Music

Sven: I tink I'm addicted to country western line dancing.

Ole: Dat's terrible. Vat are you going to do?

Sven: I'll have to go through a two-step program.

# #125 Perform in Front of an Audience

Listener: Do you take requests?

Ole: Sure, I'll give it a try. Vat vould you like?

Listener: I request you play "Far, Far Away."

# #126 Learn to Play the Harmonica

Ole: How do you know ven you have perfect pitch vit da harmonica?

Sven: It's ven you can throw it in da toilet and it doesn't hit da rim.

# #127 Try Different Kinds of Instruments

Ole: If you drop an accordion, bagpipes and a viola off da top of a 20-story building, which one lands first?

Sven: Who cares?

# #128 Learn to Play the Piano

Ole: Sven, vy do you keep banging your head on da piano keys?

Sven: Ole, don't be stupid! Haven't you ever heard of people who play by ear?

# #129 Learn to Play the Electric Guitar

Ole: Sven scares me sometimes. I told him to turn his amp on, so he hugged it, held it and told it he loved it. Uffda!

# Travel to See the World

## ☐ #130 See the Leaning Tower of Pisa

Sven: Da guy who designed dat building just had to be Norwegian.

## #131 Experience the Amazon Jungle

Lena was at the airport, anxiously waiting for her sister, Ingeborg, to arrive home from her vacation cruise on the Amazon River. As Lena saw her sister approaching, she also noticed a tall man walking arm-in-arm with her. He was dressed in feathers, with exotic markings all over his body, and was carrying a shrunken head.

Ingeborg excitedly introduced the man. "He's my husband!"

Lena gasped in disbelief. Overcome by disappointment, she squealed, "I said dat you should marry a rich doctor! A RICH doctor!"

## #132 Visit New York City

Ole and Lena were sightseeing in New York City when a mugger approached Lena. He said, "Give me all your money, lady."

Lena answered, "Sorry, but I don't have any money."

Not believing her, the mugger frisked Lena up and down. Then he sighed and said, "You're right. You don't have any money."

Lena replied, "No, but if you'll do dat again, I'll write you a check."

☐ #133 Go Whale Watching in Alaska

# #134 Visit the Vast Sahara Desert

Ole, Sven and Torvald were trekking across the Sahara Desert when they came upon a magician standing at the top of a giant slide.

The magician said, "I know you are very thirsty. To quench your thirst, you may each go down the slide asking for any drink that you would like. When you reach the bottom, you shall magically land in a giant glass of your chosen drink."

Ole went first, yelling, "Beer!" He landed in an enormous glass of ice-cold beer.

Torvald was next, and he yelled, "Lemonade!" He slid right into a giant, refreshing glass of it.

Then it was Sven's turn. As he raced down the slide, he got excited and yelled, "Wheeeee!"

# Be More Romantic

## ■ #135 Watch a Sunrise and Sunset

Ole: Da sunrise was nice, but I don't tink my
eyes can take much more of dis.

#136 Go on a Blind Date

# #137 Be a Better Boyfriend

Sven: Tina told me she vants me to be more affectionate, so I got two more girlfriends.

# #138 Fall in Love

Sven: I fell in love vit a psychic, but we broke up before we even met.

# #139 Get Married

Sven: Tina von't marry me unless I give her a ring.

Ole: Vat's wrong vit dat?

Sven: She doesn't have a telephone.

# #140 Have Children

Tina: Do you tink people should have children after 35?

Sven: No, I tink 35 is enough.

## #141 Participate in the Birth of Your Child

Ole: You'll know it's time to go to da hospital ven Tina starts yelling, "Shouldn't! Vouldn't! Couldn't! Can't!"

Sven: Ole, vy vould she do dat?

Ole: It means she's having contractions.

## #142 Go on a Romantic Getaway

Ole: I've been going on romantic getaways for years, but Lena always ruins dem.

Sven: How does she do dat?

Ole: She always makes me bring her along.

# Appreciate Nature, Part 2

■ #143 Plant a Tree and Watch it Grow

## #144 Raise Pet Fish

Ole was stopped by a game warden while leaving a lake known for its walleyes. He had two buckets of fish.

The game warden asked, "Do you have a license to catch those fish?"

Ole replied, "No, sir. Dese here are my pet fish."

"Pet fish?" the warden replied.

"Ya, sure," answered Ole. "Every night I take dese fish down to da lake and let dem swim around for a while. Den I whistle, and dey jump back into dere buckets, and I take dem home again."

"That's a bunch of hooey. Fish can't do that," said the game warden.

Ole looked at the game warden with an expression of great hurt, and he said, "Vell, den, I'll just show you."

"Okay, I've got to see this." The game warden was really curious now.

Ole poured the fish into the lake and stood waiting.

After several minutes, the game warden turned to Ole and said, "Well?"

"Vell vat?" responded Ole.

"When are you going to call the fish back?"

"Vat fish?"

## #145 Raise an Unusual Pet

Sven: Where did you get da baboon?

Monkey: I don't know. I looked down, and there he was!

## #146 Train a Parrot

Sven: If you lift da parrot's right leg, he sings "Camptown Races." If you lift his left leg, he sings "Swanee River."

Ole: Vat if you lift both legs at da same time?

Parrot: I fall off the perch, you dumbbell!

## #147 Get a Dog

Ole: I've decided to get a dog.

Sven: Ole, you've had a dog for years and years. It greets me every time I come over, and I give it a nice pat on da head.

Ole: No, Sven, dat's always been Lena.

## #148 Adopt a New Pet

A man from the big city came up to Ole's door and explained, "I'm so sorry. I just ran over your cat, and I'd like to replace him."

Ole replied, "You vould? Are you any good at catching mice?"

# Learn New Dances

**☐ #149 Learn to Line Dance**

#150 Take Part in a Flash Mob

# #151 Take Ballroom Dancing Lessons

Sven: I'm sorry. I've never danced dis badly before.

Partner: You mean you've danced before?

# #152 Learn to Tap Dance

Sven: Ole, how did you learn to tap dance?

Ole: Dat's easy. I had 14 siblings and only one bathroom.

# #153 Attend a Ballet

Ole: Lena's sister, Ingeborg, took up ballet. She was so big dat instead of a 2-2 she had to wear a 10-10.

# #154 Learn to Belly Dance

Ole: Lena is learning to belly dance.

Sven: Really, where is she taking lessons?

Ole: At da Navel Academy.

# #155 Learn to Dance in a Chorus Line

Sven: Ole, I had da worst dream of my life! I was vit twelve beautiful chorus girls. Some were blonde, some were brunettes, some were redheads. All were just beautiful!

Ole: Vy was dat a bad dream? It sounds good to me!

Sven: Oh, yeah? Vell, in my dream, I was da third girl from da end!

# #156 Learn to Be a Dance Teacher

Ole: Sven, how many dance teachers does it take to screw in a lightbulb?

Sven: I don't know, Ole. How many?

Ole: About 5, 6, 7, 8 . . .

# Self-Improvement, Part 2

## ■ #157 Relax with Yoga

Instructor: Sir, this is a YOGA class!

## #158 Improve Your Memory

Sven called Tina one morning to ask her a very important question.

> Sven: Tina, I'm so forgetful. Ven I proposed to you last night, did you say yes or no?

> Tina: I'm glad to hear from you, Sven. I knew I said, "No," to someone last night, but I couldn't remember who.

## #159 Lose Weight

> Ole: Get Lena to diet? Fat chance! Lena says dat obesity, like diarrhea, runs in her jeans.

## #160 Confess to Something You Did

> Ole: Judge, I know I've been accused of taking my uncle's change purse, but I had a good reason. You see, I hadn't been feeling vell, and I thought da change vould do me good.

# #161 Start an Exercise Program

Sven: I don't like to jog. It makes da beer fly out of da glass.

# #162 Jog a Mile Every Day

Ole: I was going to wake up early and go jogging, but my toes voted against me, 10 to 1.

# #163 Go to the Gym More Often

Sven: Da gym has no confidence in Ole. Da first machine dey put him on was a respirator.

# #164 Join a Health Club

Sven: Ole, I haven't lost any weight since I joined dat health club for $95.

Ole: How often do you go?

Sven: Vat? You mean I have to go dere too?

**Ole's Biography:** Bruce Danielson and his wife, Judy, live in Cambridge, Minnesota, with their two Miniature Schnauzers: Sam (13 years) and Toby (6 months). Bruce has taught for 39 years in New Prague and in Cambridge. He and Judy were made grandparents to the adorable Corinne Danielson in July of 2012 and enjoy any occasion they have to babysit. As he approaches retirement, Bruce has hoped for a chance to do something fun with his best friend, Bob, so he appreciates this book as an opportunity to work together as Ole and Sven.

**Sven's Biography:** Bob Bergstrom and his wife, Marj (a full-blooded Norwegian), live in Shoreview, Minnesota. Bob taught for 35 years, with the final 27 of those years at Harding High School on St. Paul's East Side, teaching ESL and International Baccalaureate (IB) English. Keeping young with the grandkids, enjoying the lake and golfing (badly) are his favorite retirement activities. Bruce and Bob have been close friends for over 40 years, after meeting as fellow National Guardsmen. They've written a play together, edited home movies together, marched in formation together and been Godparents for each other's kids, so Ole and Sven seemed like the natural (and fun) next step.